Maria Kalodaora

Cambridge Preliminary English Test 3

Examination papers from University of Cambridge ESOL Examinations: English for Speakers of Other Languages

CAMBRIDGE
UNIVERSITY PRESS

PUBLISHED BY THE PRESS SYNDICATE OF THE UNIVERSITY OF CAMBRIDGE
The Pitt Building, Trumpington Street, Cambridge, United Kingdom

CAMBRIDGE UNIVERSITY PRESS
The Edinburgh Building, Cambridge CB2 2RU, UK
40 West 20th Street, New York, NY 10011–4211, USA
477 Williamstown Road, Port Melbourne, VIC 3207, Australia
Ruiz de Alarcón 13, 28014 Madrid, Spain
Dock House, The Waterfront, Cape Town 8001, South Africa

http://www.cambridge.org

© Cambridge University Press 2003

This book is in copyright, which normally means that
no reproduction of any part may take place without
the written permission of Cambridge University Press.
The copying of certain parts of it by individuals
for use within the classroom, however, is permitted
without such formality. Pages which are copiable
without further permission are identified by a
separate copyright notice:
© UCLES K&J Photocopiable

First published 2001
New edition published 2003
Reprinted 2004

Printed in the United Kingdom at the University Press, Cambridge

Typeface Helvetica 10/13pt. *System* QuarkXPress® [OD&I]

A catalogue record for this book is available from the British Library

ISBN 0 521 75472 0 Student's Book
ISBN 0 521 75473 9 Student's Book with answers
ISBN 0 521 75474 7 Teacher's Book
ISBN 0 521 75475 5 Set of 2 Cassettes
ISBN 0 521 75476 3 Set of 2 Audio CDs
ISBN 0 521 75477 1 Self-study Pack

Contents

To the student

This book is for candidates preparing for the University of Cambridge ESOL Examinations Preliminary English Test (PET), and gives practice in all the written and oral papers. It contains four complete tests based on recent PET papers. PET tests Reading, Writing, Listening and Speaking.

PAPER 1 (1 hour and 30 minutes)

Reading
There are 35 questions in five Parts. You have to choose the right answer out of three or four options, match questions to texts or show that you think a sentence about a text is correct or incorrect.

Writing
There are three Parts: sentence transformations, a short message of 35–45 words and a letter or story of about 100 words.

PAPER 2 (about 35 minutes, including 6 minutes to transfer answers)

Listening
There are four Parts, and you will hear each of them twice. As you listen, you write your answers on the question paper. At the end, you have 6 minutes to copy your answers onto the answer sheet.

PAPER 3 (10–12 minutes for each pair of candidates)

Speaking
You take the Speaking test with another candidate. There are two examiners in the room. One examiner talks to you. This examiner sometimes asks you questions and sometimes asks you to talk to the other candidate. The other examiner listens to you. Both examiners give you marks. During the test the examiner gives you and your partner photographs and other pictures to look at and to talk about.

Preparing for PET by yourself

Reading
Have a look at some English language magazines, and read some articles about things that interest you. Look through some stories written in simplified English in your library or bookshop. Choose the ones which are interesting and just a little difficult for you, and guess the words you may not know before you look them up in your dictionary.

Writing

It can be very helpful to keep a diary in English, so that you find and learn the words that really mean something to you. You may also want to find an English-speaking pen-friend or e-pal, or to exchange letters or emails in English with a friend who is learning with you. In those letters/emails you can describe something interesting you have done, what you are doing at present or talk about your plans. In that way everything you practise will be real for you and not just an exercise.

Listening

Watch any interesting English language films at your cinema, or on TV or video whenever you can. Watch or listen to any English language teaching programmes on TV or radio. (A free list of such programmes is available from the BBC, Programme Guides, Bush House, PO Box 76, London WC2B 4PH, United Kingdom.) Listen to learning materials on cassette, so that you can hear many different kinds of voices. You may also hear people speaking English in shops, restaurants or hotels, or a tourist guide telling English-speaking visitors about places of interest in your area.

Speaking

Practise talking English with a friend who is also learning, and arrange to spend time doing this regularly. Ask each other questions, tell each other what you have enjoyed doing, talk about your daily lives, your plans, your likes and dislikes – in English. It really does get easier, once you start practising!

Further information

For more information about PET or any other Cambridge ESOL examination write to:

University of Cambridge
ESOL Examinations
The Cambridge ESOL Helpdesk
1 Hills Road
Cambridge
CB1 2EU
England

Telephone: +44 1223 553355
Fax: +44 1223 460278
Email: ESOLHelpdesk@ucles.org.uk
Website: www.CambridgeESOL.org

In some areas this information can also be obtained from the British Council.

Test 1

PAPER 1 READING AND WRITING TEST (1 hour 30 minutes)

READING

PART 1

Questions 1–5

- Look at the text in each question.
- What does it say?
- Mark the letter next to the correct explanation – **A**, **B** or **C** – **on your answer sheet**.

Example:

0

> **NO BICYCLES AGAINST GLASS PLEASE**

A Do not leave your bicycle touching the window.

B Broken glass may damage your bicycle tyres.

C Your bicycle may not be safe here.

Example answer:

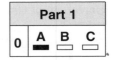

1

> *What a fantastic city. We found the restaurant you recommended but it was shut! Menu looks good value, so we'll definitely go before we leave.*
>
> Elena and Tim

A Elena and Tim have discovered another good restaurant.

B Elena and Tim think the restaurant's prices are reasonable.

C Elena and Tim will have to try the restaurant on their next visit.

2

CITY BUSES
Please have ready
the exact fare for
your journey

A All City Bus journeys cost exactly the same.

B You need to have the correct money when you board the bus.

C You must keep your ticket ready for checking.

3

☎   ☎

Frank, Rabbit Records phoned.
The CD you ordered arrived
today, but someone sold it.
They're really sorry! They've
reordered – available next
Monday at the latest.   Jan

Why did the record shop phone?

A to apologise for a mistake with Frank's order

B to suggest Frank comes in later this week

C to say that Frank's CD is ready for collection

4

The Pizza Place

Between 12 and 2 pm,
minimum charge
£3 per person

A You can buy a meal for only £3 at lunchtime.

B A charge of £3 is added to each bill at lunchtime.

C Each customer will have to pay at least £3 at lunchtime.

5

To: Dr Hatton's students
From: College secretary

Dr Hatton would like to
remind you all that
Thursday's lecture is to take
place in the library (this week
only). Start time unchanged.

A Students should check when this Thursday's lecture begins.

B Dr Hatton had forgotten to announce the change on Thursday.

C The location of Thursday's lecture will be different from usual.

PART 2

Questions 6–10

- The people below all want to see some live entertainment.
- On the opposite page there are descriptions of eight festival performances.
- Decide which performance (**letters A–H**) would be the most suitable for each person (**numbers 6–10**).
- For each of these numbers mark the correct answer **on your answer sheet**.

6  Peter is studying English. He hopes either to write plays or to be an actor. He particularly enjoys plays about real people who led interesting lives.

7  Glenda is studying the history of music at college. She wants to listen to as much music from the past as possible, and particularly likes listening to people singing.

8  Wong is a dancer from China. He would like to see people performing dances from as many other parts of the world as possible to give him some new ideas.

9  Maria is celebrating her birthday tomorrow. She wants to go out for the whole day with her friends. They all enjoy listening to pop music.

10  Ruth is a teacher who is planning to start a drama club for the children at her school. She would like to see some children acting if possible.

Summer Festival Programme

A *International Youth Celebrations*

Local youth groups, together with students from various countries including Spain, Finland, Austria and Estonia, are each performing three dance pieces. Then they will join together in a play about international friendship. The evening will finish with the singing of songs from different countries.

B *River Festival*

A day of fun on the river bank, with a Chinese theme. Street entertainers and pop musicians perform during the day, followed by fireworks in the evening. Something for everybody to watch, both children and adults.

C *Songs of Summer*

The *Hunton Consort* consists of eight voices singing music from hundreds of years ago right up to modern times. The group will perform songs, old and new, all of which are about the summer.

D *Music in the Open Air*

Well-known nationally for their traditional dance music, Jimmy Locke and his band play throughout the day in the open air on the Promenade Bandstand – if the weather allows!

E *Life Flows Between Us*

Kent Arts and Libraries present the first performance of a new dance group called the *Street Dancing Company*. The group will perform dances from the past on several of the bridges in the town.

F *A Star May Be Born*

Toni Arthur produces plays with seven- to eleven-year-olds, performed at the weekends for parents, family and friends. The plays come from children's stories, and encouragement from the audience is always very welcome.

G *Vita and Harold*

The *Image Theatre Company* dramatises the love-letters of Vita Sackville-West and Harold Nicholson. The play is about the couple's lives and their most unusual marriage. Unsuitable for children.

H *Variety Music Evening*

A great evening with the latest pop songs, and comedy and dancing from several great and unusual performers. Members of the audience will be invited to join in and will have the chance of winning tickets to a theatre show.

PART 3

Questions 11–20

- Look at the sentences below about an outdoor activity centre.
- Read the text on the opposite page to decide if each sentence is correct or incorrect.
- If it is correct, mark **A on your answer sheet**.
- If it is not correct, mark **B on your answer sheet**.

11 In August, four people visiting the centre together by car would pay more than two people.

12 The centre has activities for a range of age groups.

13 There are windsurfing courses every weekend.

14 The centre has special equipment for people who are learning to windsurf.

15 There is an extra hire charge for the board on the windsurfing course.

16 The adventure course is suitable for beginners.

17 The centre is planning to add extra facilities to the Play Park.

18 It is possible for individual visitors to stay overnight at the centre.

19 On the holiday programme children are allowed to do any sport they are interested in.

20 Summer adventure holidays are open to any child between eight and fourteen years who can swim.

The Outdoor Centre

Opening times

Water sports: 10 am – 6 pm
Play Park: 10 am – 5.30 pm

Entrance / Car park fees

Low season: Weekdays £2.00 per car   *High season:* 23 July – 11 September
Weekends £3.00 per car   Weekdays and weekends £3.00 per car

Fees are for car with four people. Each extra person is 50p. Fees to be paid at main office.

The centre is not a private club; it is an organisation whose aim is to provide outdoor sport and recreation facilities for all members of the public.

Group visitors are requested to inform the centre in advance of their intended visit.

Windsurfing — One-day course

Beginner windsurfing courses are offered on Saturdays and Sundays when the weather is good enough. Learning to windsurf is a lot of fun. The excitement when you sail across the water for the first time is not easily forgotten. Boards with small sails are available for beginners.

Course fee: *£32.50 (this includes all equipment)*

One-day adventure course

This is an opportunity you have been waiting for. Come and try sailing, climbing, surfing and archery. This course is intended to introduce outdoor activities to adults in a fun, leisurely manner. You do not need to be extremely fit or to have had previous experience of the activities. All you need is to be interested.

Course fee: *£22.50*

Play Park

The Play Park is suitable for children from two to ten years of age. It is one of the best of its type in the country. It has sand and water play, slides, large ball pool, play castle and much, much more. Next year the centre will open a new Play Palace and Play Ship.

Group day and residential courses

We also offer day and long weekend courses for groups. We receive regular visits from schools, colleges and youth groups. There are three large rooms with twelve beds in each, which can be booked in advance for groups of up to 36 people (minimum 12).

Summer adventure holidays (for 8 –14 years of age)

Sailing   **Climbing**   **Windsurfing**   **Fun Games**

Safety is of primary importance at the Outdoor Centre. All staff are fully trained in First Aid, and qualified to teach the activities on offer. We also make certain that all children only take part in activities that are suitable for their age and physical abilities. For this programme children must be able to swim 25 metres and be in good physical health.

PART 4

Questions 21–25

- Read the text and questions below.
- For each question, mark the letter next to the correct answer – **A**, **B**, **C** or **D** –
  on your answer sheet.

'The best age to start learning the violin is between three and six,' says Margaret Porter, a violinist and music teacher. 'It's the time when you are learning about the world.' Margaret, who lives in London, prefers to take pupils at three and four, although she has made lots of exceptions for keen five-year-olds. When she started teaching the violin in 1972, her first class consisted of her children's five-year-old school friends.

Margaret's pupils have group lessons. Each group has about a dozen pupils and each lesson lasts an hour, once a fortnight. In addition, each pupil has one individual lesson a week with her. Parents also have to attend the classes. It is important that the parents take an active interest in the lessons.

From the earliest lessons pupils learn to play by ear. They do not even try to read music until they have been playing for several years, and for a long time there is a big difference between their playing and reading of music. Margaret says that her method is not supposed to produce great violinists, and always suggests that pupils who perform particularly well should leave and study the violin using more traditional methods.

---

21   What is the writer trying to do in the text?

    A   explain why Margaret likes teaching the violin
    B   describe a different way of learning the violin
    C   give advice on how to find a music teacher
    D   explain why Margaret has a lot of pupils

22   Why should someone read the text?

    A   to discover how Margaret learnt the violin
    B   to learn why it is important to read music
    C   to find out about Margaret's teaching method
    D   to learn why children should play the violin

23 What opinion does Margaret have about her best pupils?

    A   They ought to find another teacher.
    B   They will become great violinists using her method.
    C   They could try harder.
    D   They take several years to learn to read music.

24 Margaret's first pupils were

    A   her children.
    B   three- and four-year-olds.
    C   her own friends.
    D   her children's friends.

25 Which of the following would Margaret include in an advertisement for her classes?

A

> **Learn to play the violin with your children – 2 lessons a week.**

B

> **Watch your children learn to play the violin.**

C

> **Group violin lessons for children – no more than 5 per group.**

D

> **We'll look after your children while you learn the violin.**

PART 5

Questions 26–35

- Read the text below and choose the correct word for each space.
- For each question, mark the letter next to the correct word – **A**, **B**, **C** or **D** – **on your answer sheet**.

Example answer:

	Part 5
0	A ■ B ▢ C ▢ D ▢

NEW OPPORTUNITIES WITH AN OPEN UNIVERSITY DEGREE

Like any other university, the Open University can **(0)** .... you a degree. However, you don't have to **(26)** .... working to study. It can also open up a whole variety **(27)** .... interests.

If you have **(28)** .... studied before, you will enjoy the special, new pleasure of **(29)** .... your knowledge. You will make friends of **(30)** .... kinds. You may also **(31)** .... that your qualification provides new career opportunities.

You don't actually **(32)** .... to the Open University for lectures, but study at home, using television, radio and computer software. You can **(33)** .... one class a month if you wish at an Open University centre. Of course, there are exams to take, as in **(34)** .... university.

If you **(35)** .... like to know more, all you have to do is complete the form below. It could be the start of a wonderful new period in your life.

0	**A** give	**B** take	**C** sell	**D** buy
26	**A** stop	**B** end	**C** break	**D** leave
27	**A** from	**B** of	**C** in	**D** for
28	**A** ever	**B** never	**C** often	**D** always
29	**A** growing	**B** changing	**C** adding	**D** increasing
30	**A** all	**B** each	**C** both	**D** every
31	**A** suggest	**B** find	**C** wish	**D** want
32	**A** join	**B** enter	**C** arrive	**D** go
33	**A** give	**B** attend	**C** learn	**D** study
34	**A** any	**B** some	**C** many	**D** most
35	**A** did	**B** will	**C** would	**D** can

WRITING

PART 1

Questions 1–5

- Here are some questions about going to the theatre.
- For each question, complete the second sentence so that it means the same as the first, **using no more than three words.**
- **Write only the missing words on your answer sheet.**

Example: The theatre has two cafés.

There *are two cafés* **in the theatre.**

1   Theatre tickets are more expensive than last year.

Last year, theatre tickets .... **than they are now.**

2   The booking office telephone is often engaged.

It is often .... **phone the booking office.**

3   Peter said, 'Why don't you go to the booking office yourself?'

Peter said, 'How .... **to the booking office yourself?'**

4   Many theatres accept credit cards.

At many theatres you .... **credit card.**

5   You can't smoke in the theatre.

Smoking .... **in the theatre.**

PART 2

Question 6

You are going to spend some time with your Scottish friend Douglas next Saturday.

Write an email to Douglas. In your email, you should

- **arrange to meet Douglas next Saturday**
- **suggest something you could do together**
- **say how long you will be able to spend with him.**

Write 35–45 words on your answer sheet.

PART 3

Answer **one** of the following questions (**7** or **8**).

Question 7

- Your English teacher has asked you to write a story.
- Your story must begin with this sentence:

  I wanted to leave the city as soon as possible.

- Write your **story** in about 100 words **on your answer sheet**.

Question 8

- This is part of a letter you receive from a pen-friend.

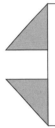

> You're keen on cooking, aren't you? What meals do you like to cook? Where do you buy all your food from?

- Now write a letter, answering your friend's questions.
- Write your **letter** in about 100 words **on your answer sheet**.

PAPER 2   LISTENING TEST   about 35 minutes
(including 6 minutes transfer time)

PART 1

Questions 1–7

- There are seven questions in this part.
- For each question there are three pictures and a short recording.
- Choose the correct picture and put a tick (✓) in the box below it. • ↘

Example: What's the time?

A ☑   B ☐   C ☐

1   What was in the woman's bag?

A ☐   B ☐   C ☐

2   Which film is the man talking about?

A ☐   B ☐   C ☐

3   What should the woman do first?

A ☐

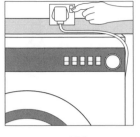

B ☐

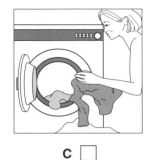

C ☐

4   What is David going to do this weekend?

A ☐

B ☐

C ☐

5   How did the man get to work today?

A ☐

B ☐

C ☐

6 Which tie does the man choose?

A ☐   **B** ☐   **C** ☐

7` What time is the appointment?

A ☐   **B** ☐   **C** ☐

PART 2

Questions 8–13

- You will hear an announcement about what's on television tomorrow.
- For each question, put a tick (✓) in the correct box.

8 *The Railway Princess* is on television from

A ☐ 9.00 to 10.00.

B ☐ 9.00 to 10.30.

C ☐ 9.30 to 11.00.

9 There is a music programme for teenagers

A ☐ early in the morning.

B ☐ before lunch.

C ☐ at lunchtime.

10 You can see a football match between

A ☐ Ireland and Spain.

B ☐ Brazil and Ireland.

C ☐ Spain and Italy.

11 If the weather is bad, there will be no

A ☐ cycling.

B ☐ skiing.

C ☐ tennis.

12   In the quiz programme, teams have to guess

    A ☐ the year.

    B ☐ the person.

    C ☐ the place.

13   What kind of film is *I Could Live Forever*?

    A ☐ a comedy

    B ☐ a musical

    C ☐ a thriller

PART 3

Questions 14–19

- You will hear a radio announcer talking about Plymouth Sea Life Centre.
- For each question, fill in the missing information in the numbered space.

Plymouth Sea Life Centre

– · – COST – · –

Adults **(14)** £ .... , children £2.00.
Special prices for over sixties and school groups.

– · – OPENING TIMES – · –

Every day except 25 and 26 December.

– · – FOR CHILDREN – · –

Special quiz.
Animals are fed every **(15)** .... from 9.30 am.
Slide and **(16)** .... shows from 10.00 am.

– · – GROUPS – · –

Guided tours available – ask at the **(17)** ....

– · – NEW ATTRACTION – · –

Walk through the big **(18)** .... made of glass.

– · – REFRESHMENTS – · –

Family area sells **(19)** .... , cold drinks, ice creams.

FOR MORE INFORMATION TELEPHONE 01743 564219.

PART 4

Questions 20–25

- Look at the six sentences for this part.
- You will hear a conversation between a girl, Jane, and her brother, Michael, about a Spanish family who are coming to visit them in England.
- Decide if each sentence is correct or incorrect.
- If it is correct, put a tick (✓) in the box under **A** for **YES**. If it is not correct, put a tick (✓) in the box under **B** for **NO**.

		A YES	B NO
20	This will be the Sanchez family's first trip to England.	☐	☐
21	Michael suggests sightseeing in London.	☐	☐
22	The Sanchez children are teenagers.	☐	☐
23	Jane has been to the car museum.	☐	☐
24	Michael thinks everyone enjoys visiting museums.	☐	☐
25	Jane and Michael have bought tickets for the tennis competition.	☐	☐

About the Speaking test

The Speaking test lasts about 10 to 12 minutes. You take the test with another candidate. There are two examiners in the room. One examiner talks to you and the other examiner listens to you. Both the examiners give you marks.

Part 1

The examiners introduce themselves and then one examiner asks you and your partner to say your names and spell them. This examiner then asks you questions about yourself, your daily life, interests, etc.

Part 2

The examiner asks you to talk about something together and gives you a drawing to help you.

Part 3

You each have a chance to talk by yourselves. The examiner gives you a colour photograph to look at and asks you to talk about it. When you have finished talking, the examiner gives your partner a different photograph to look at and to talk about.

Part 4

The examiner asks you and your partner to say more about the subject of the photographs in Part 3. You may be asked to give your opinion or to talk about something that has happened to you.

Test 2

PAPER 1   READING AND WRITING TEST   (1 hour 30 minutes)

READING

PART 1

Questions 1–5

- Look at the text in each question.
- What does it say?
- Mark the letter next to the correct explanation – **A**, **B** or **C** – **on your answer sheet**.

Example:

0

A Do not leave your bicycle touching the window.

B Broken glass may damage your bicycle tyres.

C Your bicycle may not be safe here.

Example answer:

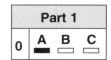

1

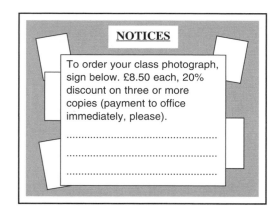

A There will be a class photo if enough people sign here.

B Your photo will cost less if you pay the office in advance.

C The price per photo is reduced if several are ordered at once.

26

2

Company Security

Office staff must have their identity cards with them at all times.

A The company insists office workers carry an identity card.

B Show your identity card when asked to do so.

C Staff identity cards are available at the office.

3

NO DIVING ALLOWED EXCEPT AT THE DEEP END OF THE SWIMMING POOL

A Swimming is not permitted where people are diving.

B You must not dive into the pool where the water is shallow.

C The water is not deep enough in this pool for you to dive.

4

Gareth

The printer's not working properly — I've put in more ink, but that hasn't helped. Can you fix it? I must print out my essay tonight!

Jasmine

Jasmine wants Gareth to

A repair the printer for her.

B help her finish an essay.

C bring her some proper ink.

5

Patients with appointments ring once and enter. Those with enquiries ring twice and enter.

A To make an appointment, ring once and enter.

B You should ring twice and enter unless you have an enquiry.

C Ring once if you have an appointment and twice if you don't.

PART 2

Questions 6–10

- The people below all want to choose a place to eat or drink.
- On the opposite page there are descriptions of eight restaurants and cafés.
- Decide which place (**letters A–H**) would be the most suitable for each group of people (**numbers 6–10**).
- For each of these numbers mark the correct letter **on your answer sheet**.

6  Mrs Jones and her daughter are going to have a day in town. Their bus arrives there at ten o'clock. They would like to have coffee before they start shopping.

7  The Browns are on holiday. They are spending the day sightseeing in town and want to have a meal at a restaurant suitable for small children. They would like to sit outside.

8  Linda's Italian friend Maria is visiting her for a week. They want to have a snack before going to the cinema in the evening. Maria is keen to try English food. Linda doesn't eat meat.

9  Robert Evans has invited a Swedish businessman to dinner to discuss a contract. He wants to take him to a restaurant near his office in the city centre. The food and service must be excellent.

10  A group of students from various countries want to go out for a late-night meal, but they don't have much money, and don't like English food!

A **The White Horse Inn** has a top-class restaurant. It is in an attractive village seven kilometres from town. Head chef Paul Grant has won prizes for his traditional English food which is served in a comfortable setting. Large garden with children's play area.

Open 10.00–14.00, 19.00–23.00.

B **The Silver Palace Chinese Restaurant** serves food from many parts of China at low prices. The atmosphere is warm and friendly, but it can get noisy. Reasonable service. Near the city centre, with a car park.

Open 12.00–14.00, 17.30–02.00.

C **Dandelions** is a small self-service vegetarian café. Serves home-cooked food including soup, pizzas, salads and wonderful desserts. Popular with office workers at lunchtime. Good value for money.

Open 11.30–14.30 only.

D **The Tiny Tea Room** serves a selection of tea, coffee and good home-made cakes and pastries. Perfect for a refreshing rest and there is a games room for children. Gets very crowded at lunchtime.

Open 09.00–16.30.

E **King's Restaurant** is a good choice for quick, inexpensive meals. This restaurant serves a wide range of English food. There is also an interesting vegetarian menu which includes a variety of hot dishes, and salads.

Open 11.00–22.00.

F **Bernini's** is a high-quality Italian restaurant. It is internationally recognised for its first-class food and service. Bernini's is close to the city centre and parking is available.

Open evenings only, 18.00–23.00.

G **The Tower Coffee Bar** serves light snacks, soft drinks and excellent Italian coffee. Its friendly atmosphere is popular with students and young people, and it is a good meeting place for friends. Can be rather noisy!

Open midday to midnight.

H **Gordon's** is a restaurant in an attractive part of town, and has tables in the garden for sunny days. It's known for pizza, fried chicken and hamburgers. Gordon's has special prices for children's meals. Excellent food but service can be slow.

Open 12.00–20.00.

PART 3

Questions 11–20

- Look at the sentences below about a club for stamp collectors.
- Read the text on the opposite page to decide if each sentence is correct or incorrect.
- If it is correct, mark **A on your answer sheet**.
- If it is not correct, mark **B on your answer sheet**.

11   The Stamp Collectors' Club sends you special stamps from many different countries.

12   The Club sends every member the same set of new stamps.

13   Information packs include a full set of stamps.

14   It costs £5 a year to join the Stamp Collectors' Club.

15   It is cheaper if several people join the Club together.

16   The Club sends each new member a hundred free stamps.

17   The guide tells you where you may be able to buy the stamps you want.

18   Members of the Club are sent a monthly magazine.

19   The magazine helps you to contact other members.

20   You must write a letter to the Club if you want to join.

STAMP COLLECTING – IT'S A HOBBY THAT CAN GROW AND GROW

Millions of people of all ages enjoy a hobby which is both interesting and fun. And every year, more and more people start a stamp collection of their own and discover an interest which can last a lifetime. Starting your collection is easy because stamps are everywhere. Holiday postcards from friends, birthday cards from favourite aunts and letters from pen-friends can all provide you with stamps from all over the world. But once you've started collecting seriously, you will probably want to join the Stamp Collectors' Club which exists to provide collectors with new British stamps.

As a Club member you order the special sets of new stamps you want for your collection. You can receive these in three different ways. We can either post you a complete set of stamps on an envelope addressed to you, or send you the same stamps in a colourful information pack with lots of interesting facts. Or, if you prefer, we can send you the individual stamps for you to arrange in a special book of your own.

The Stamp Collectors' Club has about 70,000 members and you could become a member too, with a two-year membership costing just £5. You can even get a reduction if a group of you join at the same time. We're sure you'll agree that this is great value for money.

And when you join, the Club sends you a Starter Pack at no extra cost. This contains 100 stamps to begin your collection, together with an attractive box to keep them in. You also receive our helpful 4-page guide to collecting, which has further suggestions on how to add to your collection and includes useful addresses of shops and businesses that sell stamps.

Every two months you'll get a copy of the club magazine, which is packed full of competitions and quizzes, and gives you the chance to exchange stamps with members around the world.

Why not start on an adventure which will give you years of pleasure? You'll spend many happy hours looking at the amazing variety of stamps in your collection or searching for unusual ones which you know are out there somewhere just waiting to be found. So join the Stamp Collectors' Club today and discover the fun and excitement of stamp collecting.

To join the Club simply complete the application form and send your membership fee. Your Starter Pack will be sent within 28 days of receipt of your application.

PART 4

Questions 21–25

- Read the text and questions below.
- For each question, mark the letter next to the correct answer – **A**, **B**, **C** or **D** – **on your answer sheet**.

Atlantic College

Last week I went to visit Atlantic College, an excellent private college in Wales. Unusually, it gives young people much needed experience of life outside the classroom, as well as the opportunity to study for their exams. The students, who are aged between 16 and 18 and come from all over the world, spend the morning studying. In the afternoon they go out and do a really useful activity, such as helping on the farm, looking after people with learning difficulties, or checking for pollution in rivers.

One of the great things about Atlantic College students is that they come from many different social backgrounds and countries. As few can afford the fees of £20,000 over two years, grants are available. A quarter of the students are British, and many of those can only attend because they receive government help.

'I really admire the college for trying to encourage international understanding among young people', as Barbara Molenkamp, a student from the Netherlands, said. 'You learn to live with people and respect them, even the ones you don't like. During the summer holidays my mother couldn't believe how much less I argued with my sister.'

To sum up, Atlantic College gives its students an excellent education, using methods which really seem to work.

---

21   What is the writer trying to do in the text?

    A   give an opinion about a particular student
    B   give an opinion about a special type of education
    C   describe the activities the students do in their free time
    D   describe his own experience of education

22   What can a reader find out from this text?

    A   how to become a student at Atlantic College
    B   what kind of programme Atlantic College offers
    C   what the British education system is like
    D   how to get along better with other people

23 What is the writer's opinion of Atlantic College?

    A It doesn't allow students enough study time.
    B Its students are taught to like each other.
    C It doesn't give good value for money.
    D Its way of teaching is successful.

24 Since being at Atlantic College, Barbara

    A has learnt a lot about other countries.
    B has become more confident than her sister.
    C finds it easier to get on with other people.
    D prefers her new friends to her family.

25 Which advertisement uses correct information about Atlantic College?

A

> **Study at Atlantic College.**
> **Courses for 16–18 year olds.**
> **Lessons all morning,**
> **sport in the afternoon.**

B

> **Study at Atlantic College.**
> **Courses for 16–18 year olds.**
> **Morning lessons and**
> **afternoon activities.**
> **Help with fees available.**

C

> **Study at Atlantic College.**
> **Classes on international topics.**
> **Many free places available.**
> **Students of all ages welcome.**

D

> **Study at Atlantic College.**
> **Learn English in a beautiful place.**
> **Lots of weekend activities.**
> **Help with fees available.**

PART 5

Questions 26–35

- Read the text below and choose the correct word for each space.
- For each question, mark the letter next to the correct word – **A**, **B**, **C** or **D** – **on your answer sheet**.

Example answer:

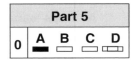

LITTLE CAT, LITTLE CAT, WHERE HAVE YOU BEEN?

When Bo the cat **(0)** .... to explore a furniture van, she had a bigger adventure than she expected. She was discovered **(26)** .... the driver, after he had completed a **(27)** .... of over 500 kilometres. It was **(28)** .... end of a long day. The driver and the cat were both hungry! He gave her some milk and started making enquiries. He telephoned his last **(29)** .... , but they had not lost a cat. It was getting late, so he took Bo home for the night and **(30)** .... morning delivered her to an animal hospital.

The cat's owner **(31)** .... done some detective work too. After **(32)** .... everywhere for the cat, he suddenly remembered the furniture van **(33)** .... had made a delivery to a neighbour. Fortunately, he **(34)** .... the name of the company. He called their office and in a short time Bo was **(35)** .... safely.

0	**A** decided	**B** suggested	**C** insisted	**D** persuaded
26	**A** of	**B** from	**C** at	**D** by
27	**A** trip	**B** visit	**C** tour	**D** travel
28	**A** an	**B** some	**C** the	**D** any
29	**A** shoppers	**B** buyers	**C** callers	**D** customers
30	**A** next	**B** following	**C** tomorrow	**D** other
31	**A** has	**B** is	**C** had	**D** was
32	**A** seeing	**B** searching	**C** watching	**D** spying
33	**A** what	**B** this	**C** it	**D** which
34	**A** called	**B** remembered	**C** saw	**D** reminded
35	**A** given	**B** brought	**C** returned	**D** taken

WRITING

PART 1

Questions 1–5

- Here are some sentences about a novel.
- For each question, complete the second sentence so that it means the same as the first, **using no more than three words.**
- **Write only the missing words on your answer sheet.**

    Example: This novel is by Joan Brady.

           Joan Brady is .the author of. **this novel.**

1   My sister has borrowed the novel from me.

    I .... **my sister the novel.**

2   She hasn't read a novel by Joan Brady before.

    This is .... **novel by Joan Brady that she has read.**

3   The novel is longer than Joan Brady's other books.

    Joan Brady's other books are not as .... **this one.**

4   How much does the novel cost?

    What is .... **the novel?**

5   I hope my sister returns the novel to me soon.

    I hope my sister .... **back the novel soon.**

PART 2

Question 6

You are on holiday in the mountains and have just bought this postcard to send to your friend Alex in Britain.

In your postcard to Alex, you should

- **explain when your holiday started**
- **tell Alex where you are staying**
- **say what you are enjoying most about the holiday.**

Write 35–45 words on your answer sheet.

PART 3

Answer **one** of the following questions (**7** or **8**).

Question 7

• This is part of a letter you receive from an Australian friend.

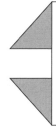

> Could you give me some advice? I want to
> travel around your country for a month.
> Where should I go? What should I see?

• Now write a letter, answering your friend's questions.
• Write your **letter** in about 100 words **on your answer sheet**.

Question 8

• You have to write a story for your English teacher.
• Your story must have this title:

A difficult day.

• Write your **story** in about 100 words **on your answer sheet**.

PAPER 2   LISTENING TEST   about 35 minutes
(including 6 minutes transfer time)

PART 1

Questions 1–7

- There are seven questions in this part.
- For each question there are three pictures and a short recording.
- Choose the correct picture and put a tick (✓) in the box below it.

Example: What's the time?

   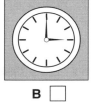   

A ✓   B ☐   C ☐

1   How did the film end?

A ☐   B ☐   C ☐

2   What time does the train to Rome leave?

A ☐   B ☐   C ☐

3 What is broken?

A ☐

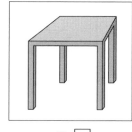

B ☐

C ☐

4 Where are the man's shoes?

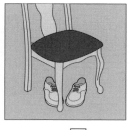

A ☐

B ☐

C ☐

5 What will Paul get at the shop?

A ☐

B ☐

C ☐

6 How were they told to do their homework?

A ☐

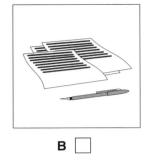

B ☐

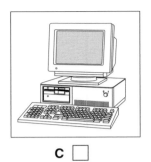

C ☐

7 What did Helen buy?

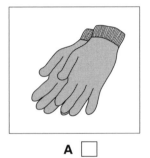

A ☐

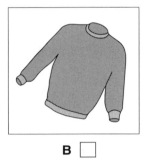

B ☐

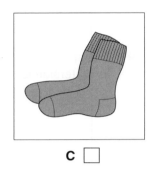

C ☐

PART 2

Questions 8–13

- You will hear part of a local radio programme in which someone is talking about a shopping centre.
- For each question, put a tick (✓) in the correct box.

8   The shopping centre opened

        A ☐ three weeks ago.

        B ☐ two months ago.

        C ☐ three years ago.

9   The speaker suggests the best way of travelling
to Waterside is by

        A ☐ coach.

        B ☐ car.

        C ☐ train.

10   On Fridays the shops are open from

        A ☐ 9 to 9.

        B ☐ 10 to 8.

        C ☐ 10 to 9.

11   On the third level, you can

        A ☐ get information.

        B ☐ watch a film.

        C ☐ find a bank.

12   Apart from shopping, what else can you do at Waterside?

A ☐ feed the ducks

B ☐ go swimming

C ☐ go sailing

13   What does the speaker complain about?   A ☐ There was nowhere to put rubbish.

B ☐ The food in the café was disappointing.

C ☐ The service in the shops was slow.

PART 3

Questions 14–19

- You will hear five messages left on an answerphone.
- For each question, fill in the missing information in the numbered space.

These messages were on the answerphone.

- **Sarah Smith** rang to say she left her **(14)** .... behind yesterday.

- **Alex** arrives about 6.00 tomorrow evening.
  Please collect him from station when he rings.
  Has lots of **(15)** .... !

- **Helen** phoned to invite you to have **(16)** .... on Saturday.
  Has friends visiting from **(17)** ....

- **Premier Travel** say holiday tickets have arrived.
  Change of departure time from 7.30 am to **(18)** .... am.
  This means 7.30 check-in!

- **Mary** called. Problem at Australian **(19)** .... Call at once. She's at home after 7.00.

PART 4

Questions 20–25

- Look at the six sentences for this part.
- You will hear a conversation between Matthew and his mother.
- Decide if each sentence is correct or incorrect.
- If it is correct, put a tick (✓) in the box under **A** for **YES**. If it is not correct, put a tick (✓) in the box under **B** for **NO**.

		A YES	B NO
20	Matthew had intended to catch the bus this morning.	☐	☐
21	Matthew thought his mother knew he wanted the car this morning.	☐	☐
22	Matthew is going to help Alan to repair his car.	☐	☐
23	Matthew needs the car next Wednesday.	☐	☐
24	Matthew's mother agrees she made a mistake.	☐	☐
25	Matthew has the car in the end.	☐	☐

About the Speaking test

The Speaking test lasts about 10 to 12 minutes. You take the test with another candidate. There are two examiners in the room. One examiner talks to you and the other examiner listens to you. Both the examiners give you marks.

Part 1

The examiners introduce themselves and then one examiner asks you and your partner to say your names and spell them. This examiner then asks you questions about yourself, your daily life, interests, etc.

Part 2

The examiner asks you to talk about something together and gives you a drawing to help you.

Part 3

You each have a chance to talk by yourselves. The examiner gives you a colour photograph to look at and asks you to talk about it. When you have finished talking, the examiner gives your partner a different photograph to look at and to talk about.

Part 4

The examiner asks you and your partner to say more about the subject of the photographs in Part 3. You may be asked to give your opinion or to talk about something that has happened to you.

Test 3

PAPER 1   READING AND WRITING TEST   (1 hour 30 minutes)

READING

PART 1

Questions 1–5

- Look at the text in each question.
- What does it say?
- Mark the letter next to the correct explanation – **A**, **B** or **C** – **on your answer sheet**.

Example:

0

A Do not leave your bicycle touching the window.

B Broken glass may damage your bicycle tyres.

C Your bicycle may not be safe here.

Example answer:

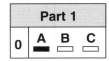

1

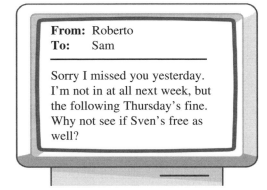

Roberto is suggesting that

A Sven is unavailable for a meeting next week.

B he will join Sam in a meeting next Thursday.

C Sam should invite Sven to their next meeting.

2

> *Need to relax after our journey – car broke down (fixed now!). At this hotel until 16th then staying overnight with Anna on the way home.*
>
> Kaye and Brian

A Kaye and Brian found their drive to the hotel stressful.

B Kaye and Brian's car needs to be repaired before they leave.

C Kaye and Brian will drive straight back after their hotel stay.

3

> # Welcome to Greenhill School. All visitors to report to school office on first floor.

A Staff must tell the office when they arrive.

B People visiting the school should inform the office.

C School reports are available in the office.

4

> Tim
>
> No more eggs left, so I'll collect some at the farm. Please buy bread in town and tell Megan to get a salad ready tonight.
>
> Mum

Tim's mother wants him to get some

A salad.

B bread.

C eggs.

5

> EVENING PERFORMANCE
> Refreshments are served only during the interval.

A Snacks are available before the performance.

B Help yourself to drinks after the performance.

C You can have a drink during the break.

PART 2

Questions 6–10

- The people below are all on holiday in Sydney, Australia.
- On the opposite page there are descriptions of eight places to visit.
- Decide which place (**letters A–H**) would be the most suitable for each of the following people (**numbers 6–10**).
- For each of these numbers mark the correct letter **on your answer sheet**.

6  Mark is an engineer and would like to spend a day looking at modern inventions and scientific discoveries. His 12-year-old daughter will probably go with him.

7  Sarah Jones and her young son want to spend a day out and see some of the animals that Australia is famous for. Sarah also wants to buy presents to take home.

8  Before she leaves Australia, Susan wants to spend a day shopping. She is looking for something special for her father, who is interested in art. She dislikes large shopping centres.

9  Mario is hoping to spend six months touring round the whole of Australia. Before setting off he wants to find out as much as possible about its history and inhabitants.

10  Stefan Holmstrom is interested in modern buildings, and always likes to get to know as much as possible about them. He also enjoys listening to music.

A

The Harbourside Development is one of the world's most exciting places to shop. It's situated right on the edge of Sydney Harbour, and there are over 200 shops, selling everything from home-made sweets to the very latest in fashion; from Australian souvenirs to Swiss watches and Japanese cameras.

B

The Australian Wildlife Park has been specially built to give people an extra close look at Australia's native animals. Have your photo taken with a kangaroo, touch and feed koala bears. There are talks every afternoon about these animals, which are only found in this part of the world. Excellent souvenir shop.

C

A visit to the Australian Museum is like an adventure across Australia. There are exhibitions on the people and their way of life, and the whole continent. Talks and guided tours help to make your visit unforgettable. There's also a café and a good bookshop, selling excellent maps.

D

The Opera House. This is a 20th century masterpiece of engineering and offers top international performances. A guided tour lasts two hours and is available any day between 9 am and 4 pm. Special 'backstage' tours are available on Sundays.

E

The State Library is in the oldest part of Sydney. There are free film screenings, guided tours and educational activities. It has regular exhibitions of books on science and technology. Learn to use a micro-computer, watch a video, or look through the Library Shop.

F

Surrounded by the modern city, the Rocks is the oldest part of Sydney and full of history. On weekends there are outdoor concerts and street theatre to enjoy. Every Saturday and Sunday there is a market where it is possible to buy the works of local artists.

G

One of the world's leading museums, the Powerhouse Museum has over 25 exhibitions on the latest developments in science and technology. Everything from a NASA space station to the first car ever built can be found at this museum. There are also many activities for children here.

H

Taronga Zoo has Australia's finest collection of rainforest birds and a sea-life centre which has many of the fish that can be found off the coasts of Australia and New Zealand. Taronga is also famous for its large group of South East Asian monkeys. Snacks are available at the café.

PART 3

Questions 11–20

- Look at the sentences below about an art gallery.
- Read the text on the opposite page to decide if each sentence is correct or incorrect.
- If it is correct, mark **A on your answer sheet**.
- If it is not correct, mark **B on your answer sheet**.

11   Children can answer quiz questions about some specially chosen pictures.

12   The Gallery has few pictures like their new one by Jan van Os.

13   It took Jan van Os a lot of time to complete his picture.

14   The Gallery had to pay a lot for the new picture.

15   The special exhibition has pictures by Spanish artists and by other artists who worked in Spain.

16   The Easter quiz is on for longer than the special exhibition.

17   In the Gallery on any Wednesday in April you can learn about 18th century Spanish painters.

18   The Gallery has just opened a restaurant for visitors.

19   A guide takes visitors round the Gallery twice every day.

20   You can see paintings from all over the world in the Gallery.

Gallery News

Easter quiz for children

During the Easter holidays young visitors can take part in a quiz on the subject of *Surprises*. The free quiz sheets can be picked up from the desk at the Orange Street entrance. Children will be directed to 14 surprising paintings and asked a variety of questions about them.

The quiz sheets will be available during normal gallery hours from 25 March until 9 April.

New picture

The Gallery now has a fine still life by the Dutch 18th century painter Jan van Os. This large picture (89.1 × 71 cm) of flowers and fruit is painted in light, bright colours on wood. It is one of the first pictures of this type in the Gallery. The picture is signed and dated 1777 and 1778. It is not unusual for a picture like this to be dated in two years: the artist waited for particular flowers to bloom in their different seasons in order to paint them. The picture was generously given to the Gallery by Miss Violet Churchman in memory of her sister Ida Nancy. It is now on display in Room 25.

Special exhibition

The exhibition 'Painting in Spain during the late 18th century' opened in the Sunley Room on 15 March. Recently the Gallery has bought works by three Spanish painters of this period: Paret, Melendez and Francisco Bayeu, who are the focus of the exhibition. These three artists are joined by Francisco's brother Ramon, by Antonio Gonzalez, and by two Italians who worked in Spain during these years – Corrado Giaquinto and Giovanni Battista Tiepolo. The exhibition runs until 31 May.

Lecture news

The series of lectures arranged to go with the special exhibition continues every Wednesday. On 5 April Lizzie Barker will discuss the work of Melendez, while on 12 April Sarah Symmons will lecture on Luis Paret. On 19 and 26 April Juliet Wilson will talk about Francisco Bayeu.

On Tuesdays in April, Erika Langmuir will explain how artists often 'tell a story' through their pictures.

Gallery restaurant improvements

The Gallery is delighted to announce that an improved and expanded service is now available in the Gallery restaurant. With its new kitchens the restaurant offers a wide choice of hot and cold dishes at reasonable prices.

Information for visitors

Free guided tours of the Gallery take place every day at 11.00 am and 3.00 pm (except Sundays). These tours introduce some of the Gallery's greatest pictures, and show the whole range of the Gallery's collection of some of the most important European paintings from the 13th to the early 20th centuries.

PART 4

Questions 21–25

- Read the text and questions below.
- For each question, mark the letter next to the correct answer – **A**, **B**, **C** or **D** – **on your answer sheet.**

When I injured my back I had to take a break from my running career. I decided to introduce more women to the sport, to show them how much fun it can be and to give them the confidence to get out and run.

I decided to start a running club for women in my area because I was annoyed by the attitude of many race organisers. They complain about the lack of women in the sport but also use this as an excuse for not providing separate changing facilities.

I put up posters and 40 women, young and old, fit and unfit, joined. All of them were attracted by the idea of losing weight but I don't think they had really thought about running before. When or if they did, they had a picture of painful training. They didn't think of chatting and smiling while running in beautiful places, like by a river.

At first they ran for only a minute – now they can run for thirty minutes. They've also learned from other runners about diet and keeping fit in general.

I wanted to do something for women's running and I've had so much pleasure watching their progress – almost as much as they've had themselves.

21 What is the writer's main aim in writing the text?

    A   to describe her own running career
    B   to complain about race organisers
    C   to talk about women runners
    D   to describe good running methods

22 What would a reader find out from the text?

    A   the best kinds of places for running
    B   how runners can avoid injuring themselves
    C   the progress made by the women in the club
    D   the teaching skills of the writer

23 What is the writer's opinion of the runners she trained?

   A   They were too serious.
   B   They needed encouraging.
   C   They couldn't develop their skills.
   D   They were difficult to train.

24 The women joined the running club to

   A   have a good time.
   B   meet other people.
   C   help them lose weight.
   D   become top runners.

25 Which of the following would be the best title for the club poster?

A
> **Discover
> the pleasures of
> running**

B
> **Riverside
> Running
> Club for
> Women**

C
> **Athletics
> competitions:
> how to win**

D
> **KEEP FIT BY
> TRAINING
> HARD**

PART 5

Questions 26–35

- Read the text below and choose the correct word for each space.
- For each question, mark the letter next to the correct word – **A**, **B**, **C** or **D** – **on your answer sheet**.

Example answer:

	Part 5			
0	A ▬	B ▭	C ▭	D ▭

MONEY

What is money? The pound, the dollar or the euro are actually just **(0)** .... a gram or a kilometre. The difference is that you can exchange money for something **(26)** .... A ten pound note may buy a book, a huge bag of sweets, or a **(27)** .... of cinema tickets. But the note itself is only a printed **(28)** .... of paper which costs almost nothing to make. Thousands of years **(29)** .... , people didn't have money as we know **(30)** .... There were no banks **(31)** .... even shops. In those days, Mr Green the farmer exchanged the corn he **(32)** .... grown for Mr Hive's honey. This was an exchange arranged between two **(33)** .... , each of whom had something that the other wanted. But in time, most societies invented their own 'currencies' **(34)** .... that people could exchange more. The different currencies began to join together, which is why **(35)** .... everyone uses the same currency in their country.

0	**A** like	**B** as	**C** similar	**D** same
26	**A** other	**B** else	**C** another	**D** apart
27	**A** couple	**B** double	**C** few	**D** several
28	**A** slice	**B** part	**C** side	**D** piece
29	**A** since	**B** past	**C** before	**D** ago
30	**A** them	**B** it	**C** some	**D** that
31	**A** or	**B** neither	**C** and	**D** but
32	**A** did	**B** was	**C** had	**D** has
33	**A** jobs	**B** people	**C** things	**D** goods
34	**A** for	**B** by	**C** because	**D** so
35	**A** tomorrow	**B** today	**C** recently	**D** soon

WRITING

PART 1

Questions 1–5

- Here are some questions about cold weather.
- For each question, complete the second sentence so that it means the same as the first, **using no more than three words.**
- **Write only the missing words on your answer sheet.**

      Example: Yesterday it snowed all day.

              It didn't *stop snowing*. **yesterday.**

1   Last year wasn't as cold as this year.

     This year is .... **last year was.**

2   How much is it to go skiing?

     What .... **to go skiing?**

3   Do you know who these skis belong to?

     Do you know .... **these skis are?**

4   James can ski well.

     James is .... **skiing.**

5   Driving in heavy snow isn't easy.

     Heavy snow makes it .... **drive.**

PART 2

Question 6

You want to invite Maria, an English-speaking student who is staying with you, to go out tonight with you and your friends.

Write a note to leave for Maria

- **inviting her to go out with you all tonight**
- **saying where you plan to spend the evening**
- **suggesting what time she should be ready.**

Write 35–45 words on your answer sheet.

PART 3

Answer **one** of the following questions (**7** or **8**).

Question 7

- You have to write a story for your English homework.

- Your story must begin with this sentence:

  The ship left the harbour at sunset.

- Write your **story** in about 100 words **on your answer sheet**.

Question 8

- This is part of a letter you receive from an English friend.

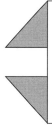
In your last letter, you said you had made some changes to your room. What does it look like now? What new furniture have you got? Tell me all about it!

- Now write a letter telling your friend about your room.
- Write your **letter** in about 100 words **on your answer sheet**.

PAPER 2   LISTENING TEST   about 35 minutes
(including 6 minutes transfer time)

PART 1

Questions 1–7

- There are seven questions in this part.
- For each question there are three pictures and a short recording.
- Choose the correct picture and put a tick (✓) in the box below it.

Example: What's the time?

A ✓   B ☐   C ☐

1   How did the woman get to work today?

A ☐   B ☐   C ☐

2   Where does the pollution come from?

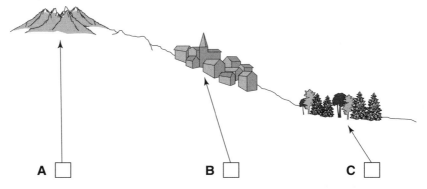

A ☐   B ☐   C ☐

3   When must the boys get on the coach?

A ☐   **B** ☐   **C** ☐

4   What fruit do they take?

A ☐   **B** ☐   **C** ☐

5   Which present has the man bought?

A ☐   **B** ☐   **C** ☐

6   Where are the photographs?

A ☐

B ☐

C ☐

7   What did Ben break?

A ☐

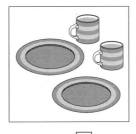

B ☐

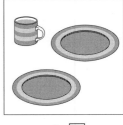

C ☐

PART 2

Questions 8–13

- You will hear a radio presenter talking about weekend events in the Carlisle area.
- For each question, put a tick (✓) in the correct box.

8   The concert starts at

    A ☐ 7 pm.

    B ☐ 7.30 pm.

    C ☐ 8.30 pm.

9   The money from the concert will pay for

    A ☐ books for the school library.

    B ☐ some school sports equipment.

    C ☐ a school trip to London.

10   The Walking Club will meet

    A ☐ in the market square.

    B ☐ at the bus station.

    C ☐ in the car park by the lake.

11   You can hear a talk by a writer

    A ☐ in the library.

    B ☐ at the bookshop.

    C ☐ at the university.

12   The writer will talk about

A ☐ a famous person she has written about.

B ☐ a recent journey she has made.

C ☐ the next book she will write.

13   To go to the talk you should

A ☐ be a club member.

B ☐ be over 16.

C ☐ book a ticket.

PART 3

Questions 14–19

- You will hear a recorded message about hotels in the National Park.
- For each question, fill in the missing information in the numbered space.

HOTELS IN THE NATIONAL PARK

The Marston Hotel

Good for people who like **(14)** ....

If you ask, the hotel will make you a **(15)** ....

The Bristol Hotel

Price includes **(16)** ....

The Ferndale Hotel

Good view of **(17)** ....

Firtrees Hotel

Has won prizes for its **(18)** ....

Price of a double room **(19)** £ .... a night.

PART 4

Questions 20–25

- Look at the six sentences for this part.
- You will hear a conversation between a boy, John, and a girl, Louise.
- Decide if each sentence is correct or incorrect.
- If it is correct, put a tick (✓) in the box under **A** for **YES**. If it is not correct, put a tick (✓) in the box under **B** for **NO**.

		A YES	B NO
20	John hopes to keep his singing lessons a secret.	☐	☐
21	John says he has had singing lessons before.	☐	☐
22	John and Louise agree that the teacher is strict.	☐	☐
23	John has always liked musical shows.	☐	☐
24	John was pleased with the practice show.	☐	☐
25	Louise would like to dance in a musical show.	☐	☐

Visual material for the Speaking test

1A

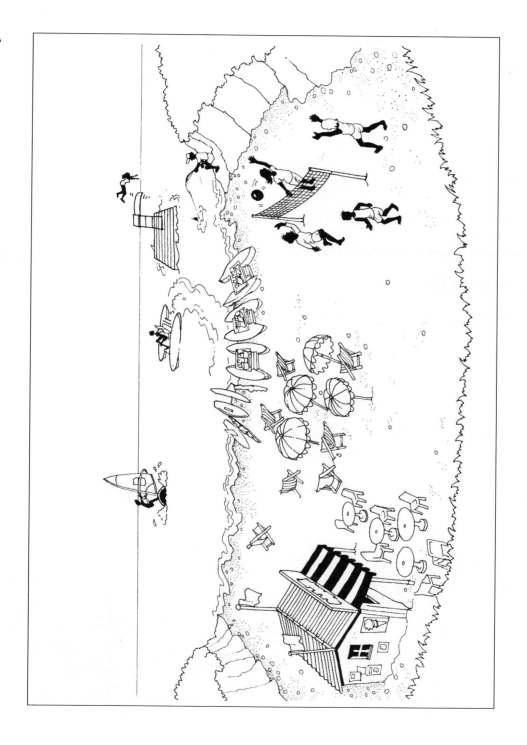

1B

2B

3B

4B

2A

3A

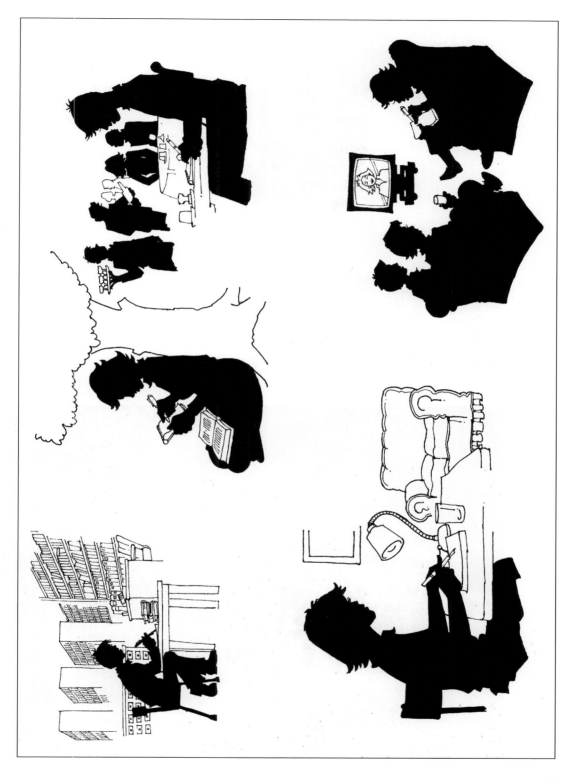

1C

2C

3C

4C

4D

4A

About the Speaking test

The Speaking test lasts about 10 to 12 minutes. You take the test with another candidate. There are two examiners in the room. One examiner talks to you and the other examiner listens to you. Both the examiners give you marks.

Part 1

The examiners introduce themselves and then one examiner asks you and your partner to say your names and spell them. This examiner then asks you questions about yourself, your daily life, interests, etc.

Part 2

The examiner asks you to talk about something together and gives you a drawing to help you.

Part 3

You each have a chance to talk by yourselves. The examiner gives you a colour photograph to look at and asks you to talk about it. When you have finished talking, the examiner gives your partner a different photograph to look at and to talk about.

Part 4

The examiner asks you and your partner to say more about the subject of the photographs in Part 3. You may be asked to give your opinion or to talk about something that has happened to you.

Test 4

PAPER 1   READING AND WRITING TEST   (1 hour 30 minutes)

READING

PART 1

Questions 1–5

- Look at the text in each question. .
- What does it say?
- Mark the letter next to the correct explanation – **A**, **B** or **C** – **on your answer sheet**.

Example:

0

> **NO BICYCLES
> AGAINST GLASS
> PLEASE**

A Do not leave your bicycle touching the window.

B Broken glass may damage your bicycle tyres.

C Your bicycle may not be safe here.

Example answer:

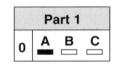

1

> **Class 9.2**
>
> Unfortunately Mr Johnstone has phoned the office to say he is delayed because of heavy traffic. Please continue with yesterday's project work until he arrives.

A Mr Johnstone will unfortunately be unable to teach Class 9.2 today.

B Class 9.2 should get on with some unfinished work for part of the lesson.

C Students who arrive late to Mr Johnstone's class must tell the office.

2

VISITORS TO THE PORT AREA MUST COLLECT AN IDENTITY CARD AT THE MAIN GATE

A It is essential to bring an identity card to the port.

B This entrance is to be used only by people with identity cards.

C To visit this area, go to the main entrance for an identity card.

3

DO NOT CLIMB CASTLE WALLS – DANGER OF FALLING STONES

A Do not climb the walls as they are dangerous.

B There is a danger of falling on to the stones.

C Check for loose stones before you climb.

4

Passengers unable to show a ticket must pay an immediate fine of £10

A A £10 fine will be payable later if you travel without a ticket.

B If you lose your ticket, a new one will cost you £10.

C You are fined £10 at once if you can't show us your ticket.

5

Mustafa, your brother phoned. He's emailed you something to read before you write that letter to the hotel. I said you'd call his mobile number today.

Jean

How should Mustafa reply to his brother?

A by email

B by phone

C by letter

PART 2

Questions 6–10

- The people below are all looking for a place to go on holiday.
- On the opposite page there are descriptions of eight places.
- Decide which place (**letters A–H**) would be the most suitable for the following people (**numbers 6–10**).
- For each of these numbers mark the correct letter **on your answer sheet**.

6  Pedro and his two friends want to spend some time in a seaside town where they can do water sports and be taught how to sail a boat properly.

7  Adriana and Claire want lots of entertainment in the evening after they have spent all day relaxing on the beach. Adriana enjoys dancing and Claire wants to see some of the latest films.

8  Pete and Elizabeth have five-year-old twin boys who are learning to swim. They want somewhere with a good beach and plenty of activities for the children to do if the weather is bad.

9  Maria enjoys going for long walks on holiday, as well as listening to music and eating good food. She prefers old-fashioned seaside places where she can really relax.

10  Susanna and Bryan and their nine-year-old son, Simon, want to go camping in a traditional seaside town, away from too many people. Simon is very interested in history.

A Ashton

The High Street, with its small, traditional cottages and excellent restaurants, is next to the stony beach where the fishermen still sell their fish every morning. There is a small cinema and popular classical concerts are held every Saturday in the Town Hall. The East Coast long-distance path passes nearby.

B Hensham-on-Sea

Hensham is a town of narrow streets with little cottages and interesting shops. There are two steam railways, one of which goes to and from the beach. Hire a boat on the small lake or go for long walks through the pinewoods.

C Brightsea

Once a fishing town, Brightsea is now a yachting centre with the best sailing on the East Coast. There are excellent walks along the river which give naturalists the chance to study the birdlife in this area. Good campsite.

D Whitecliff

A popular seaside town with lots of outside activities for everyone. The beach is a mixture of sand and small stones and visitors here have the opportunity to try windsurfing. For the very keen, there are sailing courses all the year round at the Hillstowe Sailing Club.

E Northgate

This is an attractive old town standing on the cliff top overlooking the sea. Winner of the Good Beach and Campsite prize and famous for its pleasant old streets and fishermen's cottages, one of which is now a museum of 19th-century life.

F Derringham

An old fishing port which has grown into a busy holiday town. There are good beaches but swimming is dangerous at certain times of the day. An excellent range of hotels can be found here. The town has many facilities, from museums to discos and cinemas.

G Alton Sands

A successful combination of holiday centre and fishing port. The South Beach is particularly clean and well kept. It's possible to hire a sailing or rowing boat for the day here. Outdoor swimming pools and tennis courts make this town an ideal place to spend your holiday.

H Kingsbridge

This is one of Britain's most popular seaside towns. It has wide, sandy beaches and a prize-winning Marina Leisure Centre which offers a large variety of all-weather sports, including a new swimming pool. The town has beautiful gardens along the seafront and there are interesting museums and many places to explore.

PART 3

Questions 11–20

- Look at the sentences below about Sunningdale Hotel.
- Read the text on the opposite page to decide if each sentence is correct or incorrect.
- If it is correct, mark **A on your answer sheet**.
- If it is not correct, mark **B on your answer sheet**.

11 Food is included in the cost of a room.

12 A princess used to live in the building.

13 Sunningdale Hotel is on a quiet road.

14 An *Express* bus will take you from the hotel to the centre of town.

15 The hotel provides facilities for washing clothes.

16 The hotel prefers guests who stay for a short time.

17 You can have dinner as late as 11 pm.

18 You are allowed to cook food in your room.

19 You can only play music until 11 pm.

20 It is a long way to walk from the hotel to the main railway station.

— ACCOMMODATION —

Near the town centre – Single rooms available:

SUNNINGDALE HOTEL

French, German, Spanish and Russian spoken

£200 per week single room or £36 per day with English breakfast and dinner.

Double room £160 each person per week, £33 daily.

Half price for children under 14.

The Sunningdale Hotel was built in 1913 and opened by Princess Louise. It has provided excellent service for people from all over the world and people of all ages and nationalities have stayed here. During the past 80 years over 50,000 guests from 174 different countries have visited Sunningdale.

The hotel is on one of the main roads leading to the town centre. It is about 20 minutes by bus from the centre of town and buses to many other parts of the town stop outside the hotel. Guests should be careful not to travel on buses with the blue sign *Express* on the front because they do not stop near our hotel. An underground station is less than 100 metres away.

The main building has 200 well-furnished, centrally-heated single rooms, each fitted with hot and cold water basins. Showers, baths and toilets are at the end of all corridors. The hotel has a shop, sitting rooms, four television rooms, table tennis room, library and laundry. There are also eight pianos available for guests' use. There are spaces to park cars in the hotel drive.

Daily newspapers are provided free and stamps can be bought at the office. Guests who stay for long periods must pay for their accommodation weekly in advance and one week's notice is required for departures. Short or long term guests are welcome but long term guests are offered rooms first.

Meal times are: breakfast 7 am – 9.30 am; lunch 1 pm – 2 pm; dinner 5.30 pm –7 pm. During the week, for those studying or working late, dinner can be requested until 11 pm by writing your name on the late list or by telephoning before 7 pm. A selection of 10 menu choices are available for breakfast and dinner.

No animals of any description or fires of any type (either for heating food or heating the room) are allowed, and guests are requested to respect the comfort of others. If you have tapes or CDs, please try to keep the noise level down to a minimum, especially between the hours of 11 pm and 8 am.

Guests are advised to use taxis to get to the hotel if they arrive by train because we are some distance from the main railway station.

PART 4

Questions 21–25

- Read the text and questions below.
- For each question, mark the letter next to the correct answer – **A**, **B**, **C** or **D** –
  on your answer sheet.

To: The Manager of Mezzo Mash Restaurant

Dear Sir,

Last Tuesday evening I went with two friends to your restaurant for my 18th birthday. I'd booked the table for eight o'clock and we arrived about ten minutes late, but that was not a problem. The waiter, who was very polite, showed us to our table and we studied the menu. I ordered a fish pie and my friends ordered some salads. However, after about fifteen minutes, the waiter informed us that there was no more fish pie. He apologised and suggested ordering something else. I looked at the menu again and decided to have the same as my friends – a salad.

When the food came, it was very good. After we'd finished, we decided to order some desserts. The waiter said that, unfortunately, it was too late. There wasn't enough time for us to order desserts. He said he was very sorry but our table was reserved by another group at nine thirty and we would have to leave.

We paid the bill and left feeling very disappointed. It spoilt my birthday. Nobody told us when we arrived that there was a time limit. It was very unsatisfactory and I doubt that we'll go to your restaurant again.

Yours faithfully,

Martin Cary

---

21   What is Martin Cary trying to do in the letter?

    A   make an enquiry
    B   cancel a booking
    C   make a complaint
    D   offer a suggestion

22   What will the restaurant manager discover from the letter?

    A   One of his waiters behaved badly.
    B   Some customers had a bad experience.
    C   His food is unsatisfactory.
    D   He charges too much for the meals.

23   What does Martin think about their experience?

   A   They got to the restaurant too late.
   B   There was not much choice on the menu.
   C   They won't return to the restaurant.
   D   The food took too long to arrive.

24   Martin and his friends couldn't have any dessert because

   A   someone had booked their table.
   B   they had to be home by 9.30.
   C   it was too expensive.
   D   there was none left.

25   What did Martin's friends say as they left the restaurant?

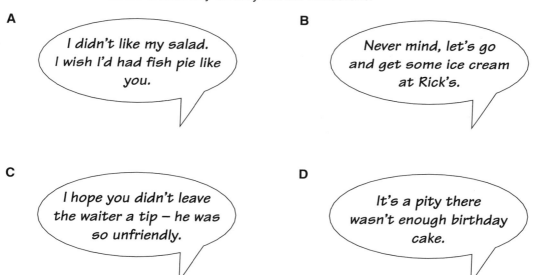

A

I didn't like my salad. I wish I'd had fish pie like you.

B

Never mind, let's go and get some ice cream at Rick's.

C

I hope you didn't leave the waiter a tip – he was so unfriendly.

D

It's a pity there wasn't enough birthday cake.

PART 5

Questions 26–35

- Read the text below and choose the correct word for each space.
- For each question, mark the letter next to the correct word – **A**, **B**, **C** or **D** –
  on your answer sheet.

Example answer:

	Part 5			
0	A ■	B ▢	C ▢	D ▢

PONY EXPRESS

Before 1860 there was no quick way of getting mail **(0)** .... the east and the west of the United States. There were no railways at that **(26)** .... and most mail was sent by coach. It usually **(27)** .... at least 25 days for coaches to **(28)** .... the coast. So in 1860 it **(29)** .... decided to send mail by 'Pony Express', which was much faster. Riders **(30)** .... very fast horses were placed along the route. They were at **(31)** .... distances from each other and the mail was handed from one rider to the next. Riders were all **(32)** .... to travel between twenty and thirty kilometres **(33)** .... day on very bad roads. At each stop two minutes were **(34)** .... for exchanging the mail bags, but riders were often held up by awful weather **(35)** .... closed the roads. With the invention of the telegraph in 1861, the demand for Pony Express disappeared.

0	**A** between	**B** from	**C** among	**D** by
26	**A** time	**B** date	**C** age	**D** season
27	**A** spent	**B** lasted	**C** took	**D** passed
28	**A** get	**B** arrive	**C** come	**D** reach
29	**A** had	**B** was	**C** has	**D** is
30	**A** for	**B** off	**C** with	**D** behind
31	**A** like	**B** equal	**C** same	**D** level
32	**A** wished	**B** wanted	**C** expected	**D** hoped
33	**A** a	**B** one	**C** some	**D** any
34	**A** let	**B** allowed	**C** done	**D** made
35	**A** which	**B** where	**C** what	**D** when

WRITING

PART 1

Questions 1–5

- Here are some sentences about a trip to the zoo.
- For each question, complete the second sentence so that it means the same as the first, **using no more than three words**.
- **Write only the missing words on your answer sheet**.

Example: Feeding the animals is not allowed.

You must not .*feed*.. **the animals.**

1 A family ticket costs £10.

The cost of a family ticket .... **£10.**

2 Entrance at weekends is more expensive than on weekdays.

Entrance on weekdays is .... **than at weekends.**

3 You don't have to pay to visit the zoo on Thursdays.

You can visit the zoo .... **paying on Thursdays.**

4 There aren't any elephants at the zoo now.

The zoo doesn't .... **any more.**

5 The new zoo restaurant has been open for a week.

The new zoo restaurant .... **last week.**

PART 2

Question 6

You have just received a present from some friends who live in the USA.

Write a card to send to your friends. In your card, you should

- **thank them for the present**
- **explain why you like it**
- **say what you are going to send them in return.**

Write 35–45 words on your answer sheet.

PART 3

Answer **one** of the following questions (**7** or **8**).

Question 7

• This is part of a letter you receive from your English friend Mark.

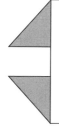

I know I spend too much time watching television! How much television do you watch? What else do you do to relax?

• Now write a letter to Mark, answering his questions.

• Write your **letter** in about 100 words **on your answer sheet.**

Question 8

• You have to write a story for your English teacher.

• Your story must have this title:

A wonderful experience.

• Write your **story** in about 100 words **on your answer sheet.**

PAPER 2   LISTENING TEST   about 35 minutes
(including 6 minutes transfer time)

PART 1

Questions 1–7

- There are seven questions in this part.
- For each question there are three pictures and a short recording.
- Choose the correct picture and put a tick (✓) in the box below it.

Example: What's the time?

A ✓   B ☐   C ☐

1   What time will the flight leave?

A ☐   B ☐   C ☐

2   Which is the photo of the girl's father?

A ☐   B ☐   C ☐

3   What must the woman wear at work?

A ☐   B ☐   C ☐

4   Where will they sit in the theatre?

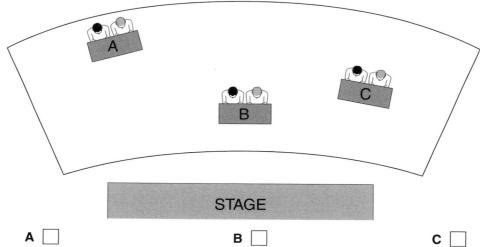

A ☐   B ☐   C ☐

5   How did the woman cook the onions?

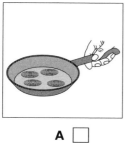      

A ☐   B ☐   C ☐

6 What will the man buy?

A ☐

B ☐

C ☐

7 How will they travel to Edinburgh?

A ☐

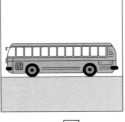

B ☐

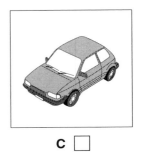

C ☐

PART 2

Questions 8–13

- You will hear someone talking to a group of students about a visit to an Arts Centre.
- For each question, put a tick (✓) in the correct box.

8   There are still tickets for

     A ☐   the piano concert.

     B ☐   *Twelfth Night.*

     C ☐   *Spider and Rose.*

9   The coach will leave at 3.30 because

     A ☐   they don't want to miss the shows.

     B ☐   they want free time at the Arts Centre.

     C ☐   it's a long journey to the Arts Centre.

10   You have to pay to see

     A ☐   the Russian ballet exhibition.

     B ☐   the Scottish jewellery.

     C ☐   the South American photographs.

11   You can buy clothes

     A ☐   on the first floor.

     B ☐   in the souvenir shop.

     C ☐   close to the Arts Centre.

12 If you want a snack and a hot drink, try

    A ☐ the Fountain.

    B ☐ Charlie's.

    C ☐ the cinema kiosk.

13 Everyone should get back on the coach at

    A ☐ 10.10.

    B ☐ 10.15.

    C ☐ 10.20.

PART 3

Questions 14–19

- You will hear someone talking about a sports camp for children.
- For each question, fill in the missing information in the numbered space.

SUNNINGTON SPORTS CAMP

Choice of afternoon activity

Sign list outside **(14)** .... room

Clothes

Wear track suit, but also bring **(15)** ....

and a T-shirt

2 pairs of sports **(16)** ....

Food

Lunch served in canteen every half-hour between

12.15 and **(17)** ....

Snack bar sells drinks, chocolate and

(18) ....

Certificate

Marks given for

attitude: effort and team-work

performance: strength, **(19)** .... and skill

---

PART 4

Questions 20–25

- Look at the six sentences for this part.
- You will hear a conversation between a young man, Mike, and his sister, Ann.
  They are talking about buying a wedding present for some friends of theirs.
- Decide if each sentence is correct or incorrect.
- If it is correct, put a tick (✓) in the box under **A** for **YES**. If it is not correct, put a tick (✓) in the box under **B** for **NO**.

		A YES	B NO
20	Mike likes to plan ahead more than Ann does.	☐	☐
21	Ann thinks they should buy a useful present.	☐	☐
22	Mike thinks he should choose the present.	☐	☐
23	Mike has known Tony the longest.	☐	☐
24	Mike thinks he will enjoy the wedding.	☐	☐
25	Ann prefers large weddings.	☐	☐

About the Speaking test

The Speaking test lasts about 10 to 12 minutes. You take the test with another candidate. There are two examiners in the room. One examiner talks to you and the other examiner listens to you. Both the examiners give you marks.

Part 1

The examiners introduce themselves and then one examiner asks you and your partner to say your names and spell them. This examiner then asks you questions about yourself, your daily life, interests, etc.

Part 2

The examiner asks you to talk about something together and gives you a drawing to help you.

Part 3

You each have a chance to talk by yourselves. The examiner gives you a colour photograph to look at and asks you to talk about it. When you have finished talking, the examiner gives your partner a different photograph to look at and to talk about.

Part 4

The examiner asks you and your partner to say more about the subject of the photographs in Part 3. You may be asked to give your opinion or to talk about something that has happened to you.

Sample answer sheets

UNIVERSITY *of* **CAMBRIDGE**
ESOL Examinations

S A M P L E

Candidate Name
If not already printed, write name
in CAPITALS and complete the
Candidate No. grid (in pencil).

Candidate Signature

Examination Title

Centre

Supervisor:
If the candidate is ABSENT or has WITHDRAWN shade here

Centre No.

Candidate No.

Examination
Details

0	0	0	0
1	1	1	1
2	2	2	2
3	3	3	3
4	4	4	4
5	5	5	5
6	6	6	6
7	7	7	7
8	8	8	8
9	9	9	9

PET Paper 1 Reading and Writing Candidate Answer Sheet 1

Instructions

Use a PENCIL (B or HB).

Rub out any answer you want to change with an eraser.

For **Reading:**
Mark ONE letter for each question.
For example, if you think **A** is the right answer to the
question, mark your answer sheet like this:

Part 1

1	A B C
2	A B C
3	A B C
4	A B C
5	A B C

Part 2

6	A B C D E F G H
7	A B C D E F G H
8	A B C D E F G H
9	A B C D E F G H
10	A B C D E F G H

Part 3

11	A B
12	A B
13	A B
14	A B
15	A B
16	A B
17	A B
18	A B
19	A B
20	A B

Part 4

21	A B C D
22	A B C D
23	A B C D
24	A B C D
25	A B C D

Part 5

26	A B C D
27	A B C D
28	A B C D
29	A B C D
30	A B C D
31	A B C D
32	A B C D
33	A B C D
34	A B C D
35	A B C D

Continue on the other side of this sheet ➡

© UCLES/K&J   Photocopiable

S A M P L E

For **Writing (Parts 1 and 2):**

Write your answers clearly in the spaces provided.

Part 1: Write your answers below.	Do not write here
1	1 1 0
2	1 2 0
3	1 3 0
4	1 4 0
5	1 5 0

Part 2 (Question 6): Write your answer below.

Put your answer to Writing Part 3 on Answer Sheet 2 ➡

© UCLES/K&J   Photocopiable

UNIVERSITY *of* **CAMBRIDGE**
ESOL Examinations

S A M P L E

Candidate Name
If not already printed, write name
in CAPITALS and complete the
Candidate No. grid (in pencil).

Candidate Signature

Examination Title

Centre

Supervisor:
If the candidate is ABSENT or has WITHDRAWN shade here ▭

Centre No.

Candidate No.

Examination
Details

0	0	0	0
1	1	1	1
2	2	2	2
3	3	3	3
4	4	4	4
5	5	5	5
6	6	6	6
7	7	7	7
8	8	8	8
9	9	9	9

PET Paper 1 Reading and Writing   Candidate Answer Sheet 2

Candidate Instructions:

**Write your answer to Writing Part 3
on the other side of this sheet.**

⟶

Use a PENCIL (B or HB).

This section for use by FIRST Examiner only

Mark:

| 0 | 1.1 | 1.2 | 1.3 | 2.1 | 2.2 | 2.3 | 3.1 | 3.2 | 3.3 | 4.1 | 4.2 | 4.3 | 5.1 | 5.2 | 5.3 |

Examiner Number:

	0 1 2 3 4 5 6 7 8 9
	0 1 2 3 4 5 6 7 8 9
	0 1 2 3 4 5 6 7 8 9
	0 1 2 3 4 5 6 7 8 9

© UCLES/K&J   Photocopiable

S A M P L E

Part 3: Mark the number of the question you are answering here ➡ $\underset{=}{Q7}$ or $\underset{=}{Q8}$

Write your answer below.

_____

_____

_____

_____

_____

_____

_____

_____

_____

_____

_____

_____

_____

_____

_____

_____

_____

_____

Do not write below this line

This section for use by SECOND Examiner only

Mark:

| 0 | 1.1 | 1.2 | 1.3 | 2.1 | 2.2 | 2.3 | 3.1 | 3.2 | 3.3 | 4.1 | 4.2 | 4.3 | 5.1 | 5.2 | 5.3 |

Examiner Number:

	0 1 2 3 4 5 6 7 8 9
	0 1 2 3 4 5 6 7 8 9
	0 1 2 3 4 5 6 7 8 9
	0 1 2 3 4 5 6 7 8 9

© UCLES/K&J Photocopiable

UNIVERSITY *of* CAMBRIDGE
ESOL Examinations

S A M P L E

Candidate Name
If not already printed, write name
in CAPITALS and complete the
Candidate No. grid (in pencil).

Candidate Signature

Examination Title

Centre

Supervisor:
If the candidate is ABSENT or has WITHDRAWN shade here ▭

Centre No.

Candidate No.

Examination Details

0	0	0	0
1	1	1	1
2	2	2	2
3	3	3	3
4	4	4	4
5	5	5	5
6	6	6	6
7	7	7	7
8	8	8	8
9	9	9	9

PET Paper 2 Listening Candidate Answer Sheet

You must transfer all your answers from the Listening Question Paper to this answer sheet.

Instructions

Use a PENCIL (B or HB).

Rub out any answer you want to change with an eraser.

For **Parts 1, 2** and **4**:
Mark ONE letter for each question.
For example, if you think **A** is the right answer to the
question, mark your answer sheet like this:

0 | A̶ ▭ C

For **Part 3**:
Write your answers clearly in the spaces next
to the numbers (14 to 19) like this:

0 | example

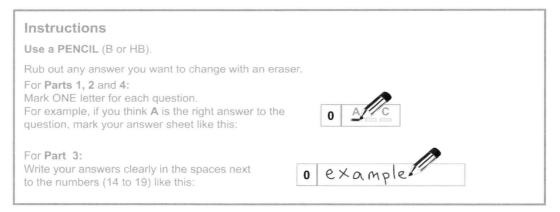

Part 1		Part 2		Part 3		Do not write here		Part 4	
1	A B C	**8**	A B C	**14**		1 14 0	**20**	A B
2	A B C	**9**	A B C	**15**		1 15 0	**21**	A B
3	A B C	**10**	A B C	**16**		1 16 0	**22**	A B
4	A B C	**11**	A B C	**17**		1 17 0	**23**	A B
5	A B C	**12**	A B C	**18**		1 18 0	**24**	A B
6	A B C	**13**	A B C	**19**		1 19 0	**25**	A B
7	A B C								

© UCLES/K&J   Photocopiable

Acknowledgements

The publishers are grateful to the following for permission to reproduce copyright material. While every endeavour has been made, it has not been possible to identify the sources of all material used and in such cases the publishers would welcome information from copyright sources. Apologies are expressed for any omissions.

For permission to reproduce photographs:

John Birdsall Photography p. II (1B); Comstock Photolibrary pp. III (4B), VII (4C); Greg Evans International Photolibrary/Greg Balfour Evans p. II (2B); Getty Images/Stone/Ian Shaw p. VI (1C), /Oliver Benn p. VI (2C), /Paula Bronstein p. VII (3C), /Walter Hodges p. VIII (4D); ImageState/Pictor p. III (3B).

Picture clearance by Hilary Fletcher

Illustrations by Chartwell Illustrators and Oxford Designers & Illustrators

Design concept by Peter Ducker MSTD

Cover design by Dunne & Scully

The cassettes/CDs which accompany this book were recorded at Studio AVP, London.